The Publishers gratefully acknowledge assistance provided by Dr Chris Packet, Acting-up Senior Sibling of CAIN (the Consanguine Aggression Information Network) in preparing this book.

Publishers: Ladybird Books Ltd., Loughborough

Printed in England. If wet, Italy.

'How it works'

THE BROTHER

by J.A. HAZELEY, N.S.F.W.
and J.P. MORRIS, O.M.G.

(Authors of 'Decorating With Wasps')

A LADYBIRD BOOK FOR GROWN-UPS

This is a brother.

He shares half of his DNA with you.

But he will not share any of his bubble mixture.

Ken will come to regret this in approximately 2048 when he needs to borrow £200 from Joy to get his van through its MOT.

Ken.

Aisling has a butterfly book.

Ryan has a book about fish.

Ryan has decided this is not fair for a reason that will become no clearer over the next six days of his going on and on about it.

FISH

Brandon's sister wants her coat back but he is keeping it because he knows how much it annoys her.

Jumping off things. Sliding down things. Drinking magic potions made of vinegar and mud. Going over there and punching Dean Haggett.

There are plenty of things which an older brother can persuade a younger brother or sister to be the first to try.

Jessica has taught her little brother Trevor everything she knows.

If he ever makes a career out of rude armpit sounds and stealing sugar sachets from cafés, she hopes he will remember who it was who got him there.

Angus is the big brother. He always has the best toys.

Hayley is the little sister. She has lots of toys, but they are broken and used to belong to Angus.

Their brother Christian is sitting in the cupboard under the stairs with a paper bag on his head waiting for anyone to notice.

Middle children are different.

SCRAP

Abel has been singing the same song over and over again the whole way from Megiddo to the Plain of Jezreel.

He also keeps putting his arm on Cain's side of the donkey.

Brothers can be very irritating but it is ever so important to try and keep your temper.

Rollo is watching his brother on the news.

"I could have done that," says Rollo to his girlfriend.

"If they'd just bought me that spacehopper."

UNITED
STATES

At home, Lucas and his sister Mia play together all the time.

But in front of his friends, Lucas pretends girls are stupid.

Their mum worries that the design of the local soft–play centre is not helping.

Music–making is easy when you are brothers like these Everly Brothers.

Phil knows what Don is thinking. Don knows what Phil is thinking.

Don is thinking, “I hate you”. Phil is also thinking, “I hate you”.

Two brothers in perfect harmony.

Joshua's sister Christine got a new bike for Christmas.

Joshua got book tokens.

"But your sister doesn't like books," says Joshua's mum.

Joshua wished he'd worked harder on looking pig ignorant in front of his parents.

POLICE

Jenny is definitely telling Mum about this.

Finbar's sister Mary is on a picnic with her new boyfriend.

Finbar staked out a commanding position above the picnic area this morning. He has not met Mary's new boyfriend yet, but if the man's poor coleslaw etiquette leads to further unacceptable behaviour, Finbar is ready to act.

Hereward is not just Sam's big brother. He is also his best friend.

Hereward will support Sam in everything he does. He will be there for him no matter what. He will always give advice and encouragement.

Provided Sam does ever so slightly worse than him at everything.

38
17

Gavin is repeating everything his big brother Tom says, but in the voice of Zippy from Rainbow.

He has also prepared a story about Tom wetting his pants at Jack and the Beanstalk when he danced with the cow.

Tom's new girlfriend will be here in ten minutes. Gavin is ready.

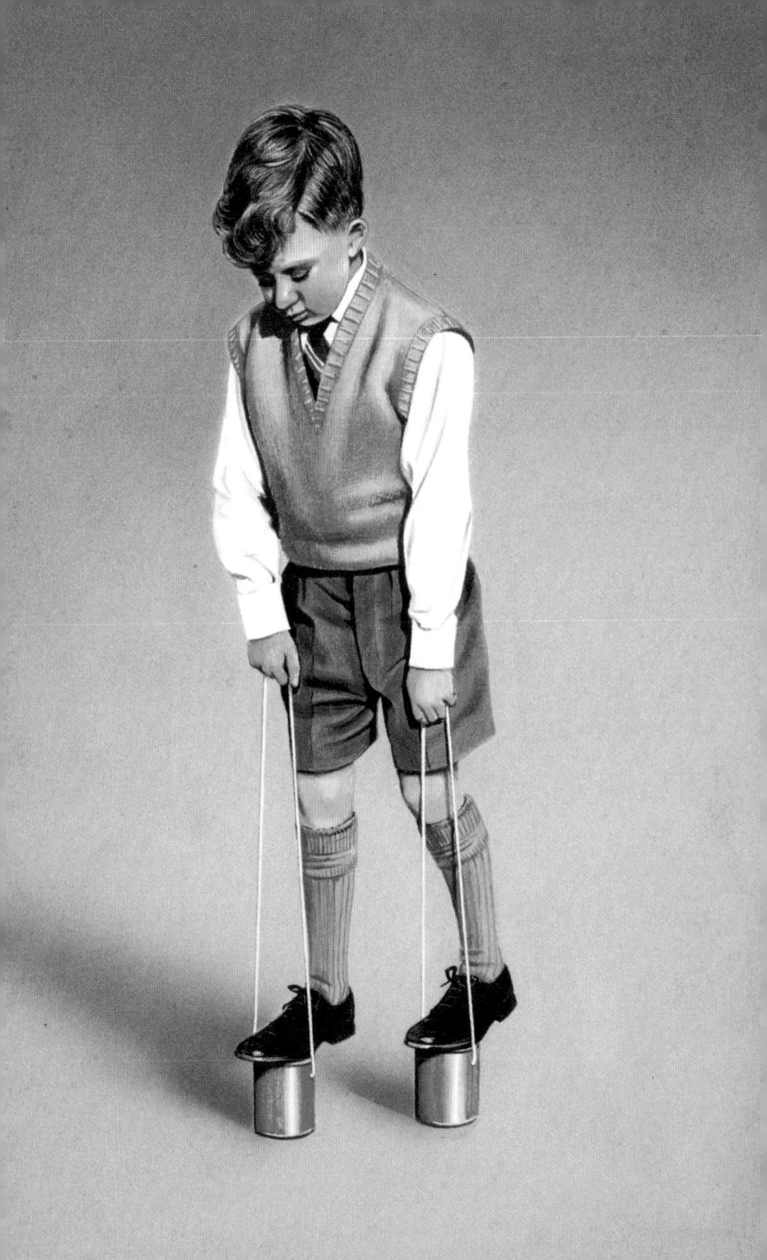

Despite being a county–class hammer thrower, Tarragon has not been asked to open the school fete.

Once again, he suspects the only reason he was allowed on the PTA committee was to invite one of his brothers to open it.

Sometimes it is tough being a Dimbleby.

When Mike visits his big brother Dan, he always gets a parcel of things to take home with him.

"I don't really need this stuff any more. Have the lot," says Dan, generously.

When he gets back to his flat, Mike will put the VHS cassettes in the charity shop, the off–cuts of MDF in the shed and all the potato peelings in the bin.

Everett is writing his memoirs.

He knows he wants to mention his time as a prisoner of war, and his music career, and his work as a neurosurgeon, and what it was like at the earth's core.

But mainly he wants to settle an argument he once had with his brother about Gary Neville.

Chang–Chang is sad.

To stop his species becoming extinct, he is probably, at some point, going to have to be nice to his sister.

Chris did not know that his lonely old neighbour, Humbert, had any brothers or sisters.

When Humbert became too ill to leave his forty–six–room mansion, Chris looked in on Humbert and got his shopping. Chris arranged the funeral and even offered to carry Humbert's coffin.

But he does not need to. There are suddenly lots and lots of long–lost brothers and sisters who are very keen to help.

Every birthday, Lee and his brother Wayne re–gift the amusing present that Lee gave Wayne when he was six. It is a running joke.

Lee and Wayne suspect their joke stopped being funny some years ago, but they are carrying on because they are brothers, and not carrying on would indicate something terrible that they can neither explain nor consider.

Also, it is easier than finding an actual present.

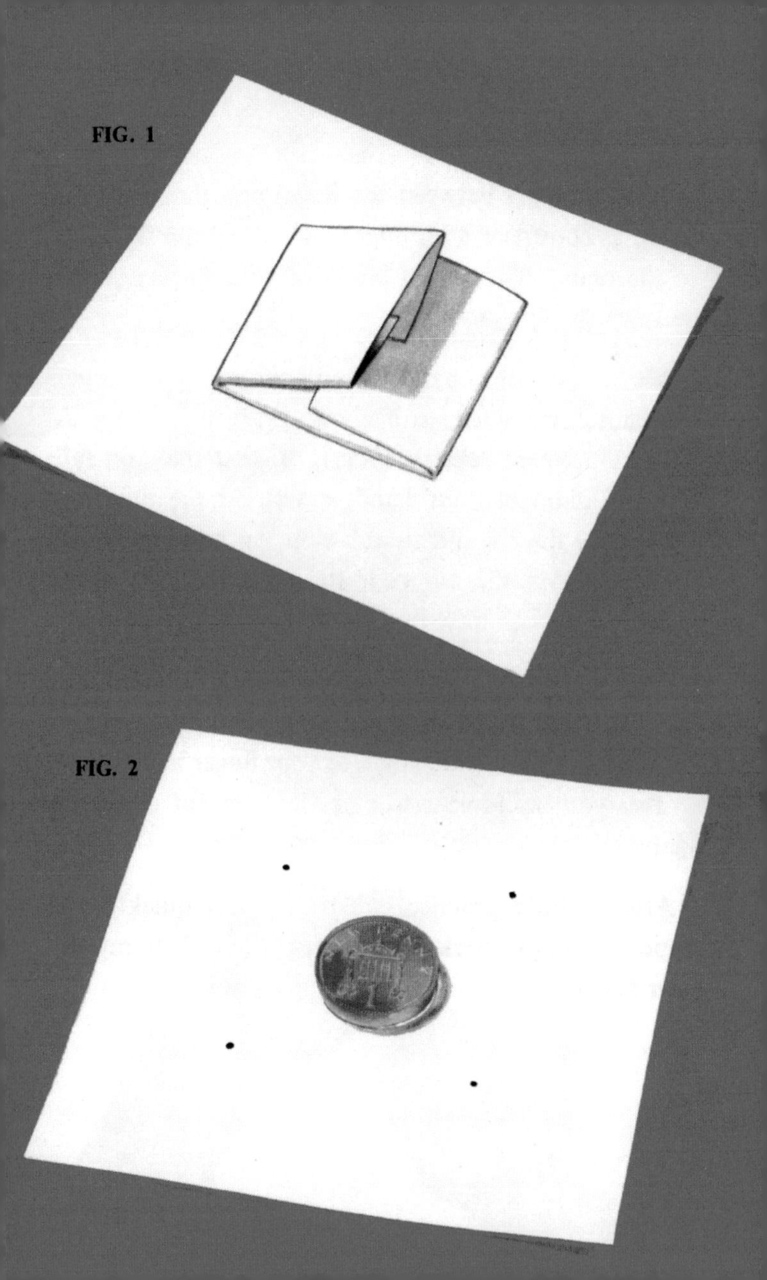

FIG. 1

FIG. 2

Caspar's parents have decided he is "the musical one", so he must practise every day after school.

Caspar is cross because his brother Ludwig gets to play in the garden instead. Ludwig is "the sporty one".

The Beethoven family have great hopes for their boys.

Adrian is explaining that he will not give his sister Lucy any of his bone marrow if she ever needs it.

Not until she gives him back the Fine Young Cannibals single she borrowed in 1989.

"It's not the bone marrow," says Adrian. "It's the principle."

THE AUTHORS would like to record their gratitude and offer their apologies to the many Ladybird artists whose luminous work formed the glorious wallpaper of countless childhoods. Revisiting it for this book as grown-ups has been a privilege.

MICHAEL JOSEPH

UK | USA | Canada | Ireland | Australia
India | New Zealand | South Africa

Michael Joseph is part of the Penguin Random House group of companies whose addresses can be found at global.penguinrandomhouse.com

First published 2017
002

Printed in Italy by L.E.G.O. S.p.A

A CIP catalogue record for this book is available from the British Library

ISBN: 978–0–718–18869–6

www.greenpenguin.co.uk